Leroy Moore

easterseals

CHERRY LAKE PRESS

Published in the United States of America by Cherry Lake Publishing Group
Ann Arbor, Michigan
www.cherrylakepublishing.com

Reading Adviser: Beth Walker Gambro, MS, Ed., Reading Consultant, Yorkville, IL
Book Designer: Jennifer Wahi
Illustrator: Jeff Bane
Graphic novel cover art, pages 15, 23: Jen White-Johnson and Asian Robles

Photo Credits: © Johnb Atherton/Flickr (CC BY-SA 2.0), 5; © Atlasfotoreception/Dreamstime.com, 7; © your/
Shutterstock, 9; © Shaiith/Shutterstock, 11; © Tom Olin, 13, 22; © Leroy Moore, 15, 21, 23; © Pressmaster/
Shutterstock, 17; © wellphoto/Shutterstock, 19

Cherry Lake Press is an imprint of Cherry Lake Publishing Group.

Library of Congress Cataloging-in-Publication Data

Names: Bertrand-Essington, Tiernan, author. | Bane, Jeff, 1957-
   illustrator.
Title: Leroy Moore / by Tiernan Bertrand-Essington ; illustrated by Jeff
   Bane.
Description: Ann Arbor, Michigan : Cherry Lake Publishing Group, [2023] |
   Series: My itty-bitty bio | Audience: Grades K-1 | Summary: "Emmy
   award-winner Leroy Moore, Jr. founded the Krip-Hop Nation, a hip-hop
   movement for people with disabilities. This biography for early readers
   examines his life and impact in a simple, age-appropriate way that helps
   young readers develop word recognition and reading skills. Developed in
   partnership with Easterseals and written by a member of the disability
   community, this title helps all readers learn from those who make a
   difference in our world. The My Itty-Bitty Bio series celebrates
   diversity, inclusion, and the values that readers of all ages can aspire
   to"-- Provided by publisher.
Identifiers: LCCN 2023009101 | ISBN 9781668927281 (hardcover) | ISBN
   9781668928332 (paperback) | ISBN 9781668929803 (ebook) | ISBN
   9781668931288 (pdf)
Subjects: LCSH: Moore, Leroy, 1967- | People with disabilities--Biography.
   | Musicians with disabilities--Biography. | Hip-hop.
Classification: LCC HV1569.3.M55 B43 2023 | DDC
   305.9/0808996073--dc23/eng/20230512
LC record available at https://lccn.loc.gov/2023009101

Printed in the United States of America
Corporate Graphics

Special thanks to Leroy Moore for his time and participation in the development of this book.

About the author: Tiernan Bertrand-Essington is a writer living in Los Angeles, California. He is an ally to the disability community.

About the illustrator: Jeff Bane and his two business partners own a studio along the American River in Folsom, California, home of the 1849 Gold Rush. When Jeff's not sketching or illustrating for clients, he's either swimming or kayaking in the river to relax.

About our partnership: This title was developed in partnership with Easterseals to support its mission of empowering people with disabilities. Through their national network of affiliates, Easterseals provides essential services and on-the-ground supports to more than 1.5 million people each year.

I was born in 1967. I lived in New York City. My dad was an **activist**.

I have **cerebral palsy**. It is a **disability**. It makes moving hard.

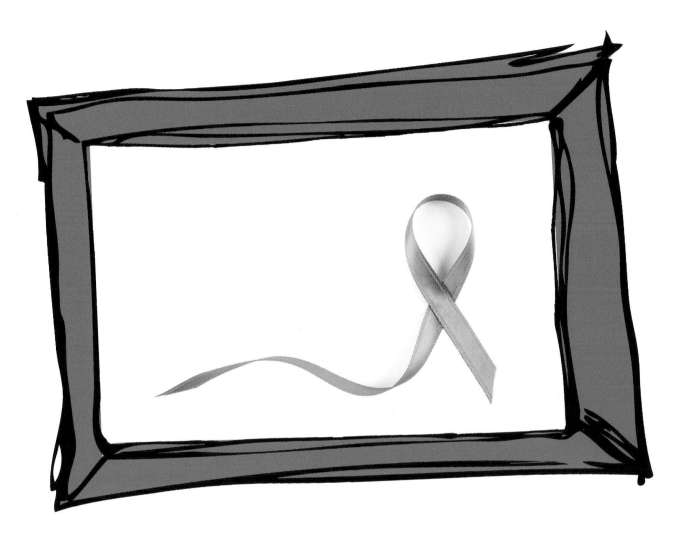

Being a kid was hard. I was different.

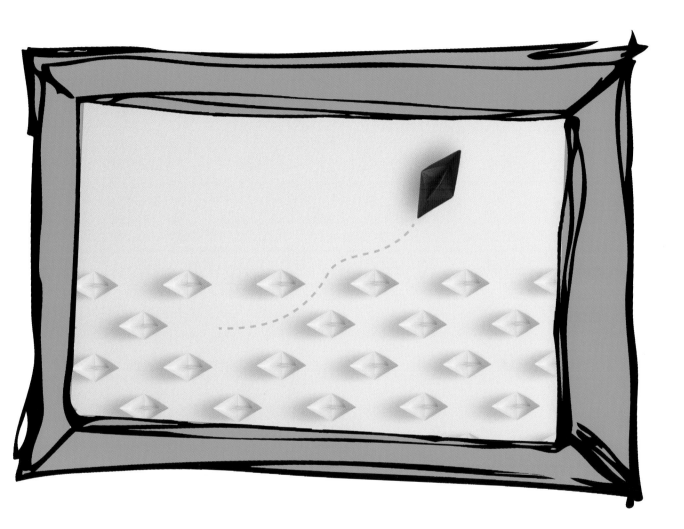

I loved poetry. I loved music. They helped. I liked hip-hop best.

What music do you like?

I grew up. I made music. I wrote poems. I spoke out. I met other artists.

I created Krip-Hop Nation. It is a group of artists. The artists are **disabled**.

We are all different. We celebrate each other. We are proud.

What are you proud of?

We honor disabled people.
We honor Black men. We help.
We teach. We work for **justice**.

Today, I write books. I write poems. I make music. I make movies.

I speak out. I work for change.

What would you like to ask me?

2007

1960

↑
Born
1967

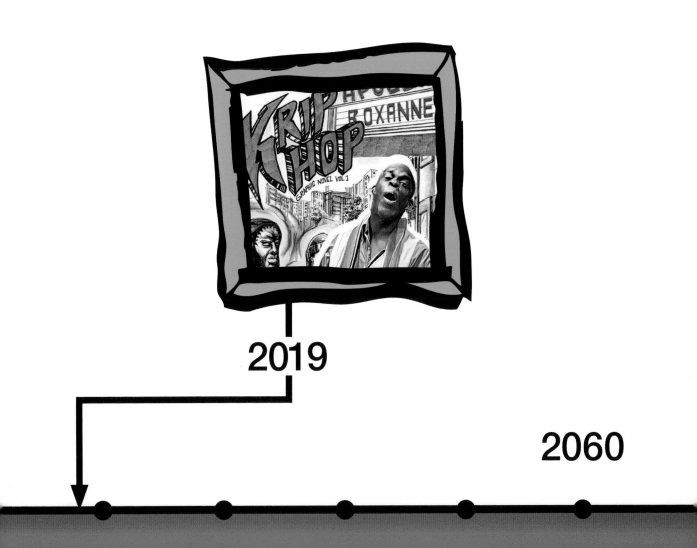

2019

2060

glossary

activist (ACT-uh-vist) one who works for a change, especially a political change

cerebral palsy (suh-REE-brull PAUL-zee) a condition some children are born with that can make it hard for them to stand up straight or move around

disability (DIS-uh-bil-uh-tee) a condition that limits a person's movement, senses, or activities

disabled (DIS-ay-buhld) having limited movement, senses, or activities

justice (JUS-tuhs) fairness

index